We want to know what you think!

Please leave a review on Amazon, Walmart, Target, Barnes & Nobles, or any other retailer where you purchased this product.

About Unabashed Kids Media

Unabashed Kids Media is a children's media brand focused on academic and social-emotional education.

Content created by Unabashed Kids Media is meant to aid parents, teachers, and educators in enhancing the academic, creative, and social skills of young children.

We publish picture books, academic worksheets, games, and storytelling media content.

Follow us on Instagram @unabashed_kids

UnabashedKids.com/blog

Unabashed Kids *Media*

Visit
UnabashedKids.com
for FREE worksheets

cat and snowman

Purchase our Christmas coloring
workbook on Amazon.

Please use **coloring pencils** and **crayons** to prevent bleed-through from markers.

KWANZAA

Kwanzaa

The word Kwanzaa comes from the Swahili saying "matunda ya kwanza" which means "first fruits". Kwanzaa is a 7 night African American celebration held at the end of each year, starting December 26th and ending January 1st. Kwanzaa was developed in 1966. In 1997 President Bill Clinton issued a public declaration marking the holiday.

Each family celebrates Kwanzaa differently, but celebrations often include songs, dances, African drums, storytelling, poetry, and a large traditionally African American meal.

KWANZAA

Kinara: The Candleholder

On each of the 7 nights, a child lights one of the candles on the Kinara. A Kinara is a special candleholder used during Kwanzaa.

The kinara is the center of Kwanzaa setting and represents ancestry. The mishumaa saba (3 red, 3 green, 1 black candle) are placed in the Kinara.

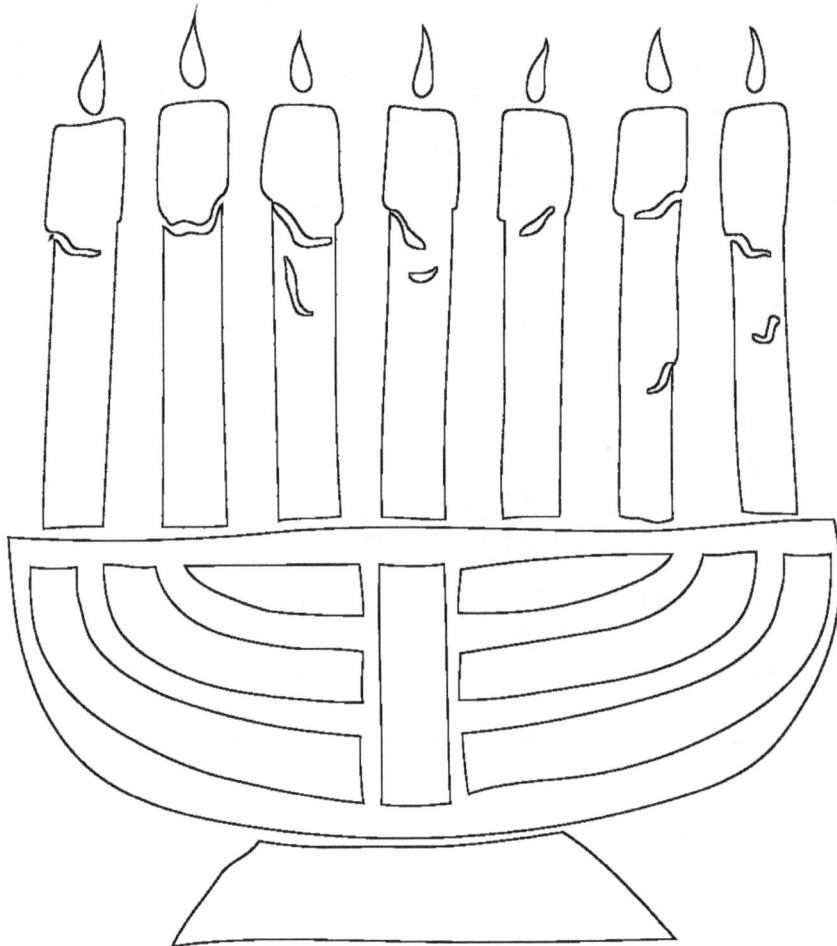

Kinara

Mishumaa Saba:
The Seven Candles

Candles are ceremonial objects with two primary purposes: to recreate symbolically the sun's power and to provide light.

Mishumaa Saba is the seven candles that represent the 7 principles: three red, three green, and one black. The black candle symbolizes Umoja (unity) and is lit on December 26th. The 3 green candles represent Nia, Ukima, and Imani; these candles are placed on the right side of Umoja candles. The three red candles represent Kujichagulia, Ujamaa, and Kuumba are placed on the left of the Umoja candle.

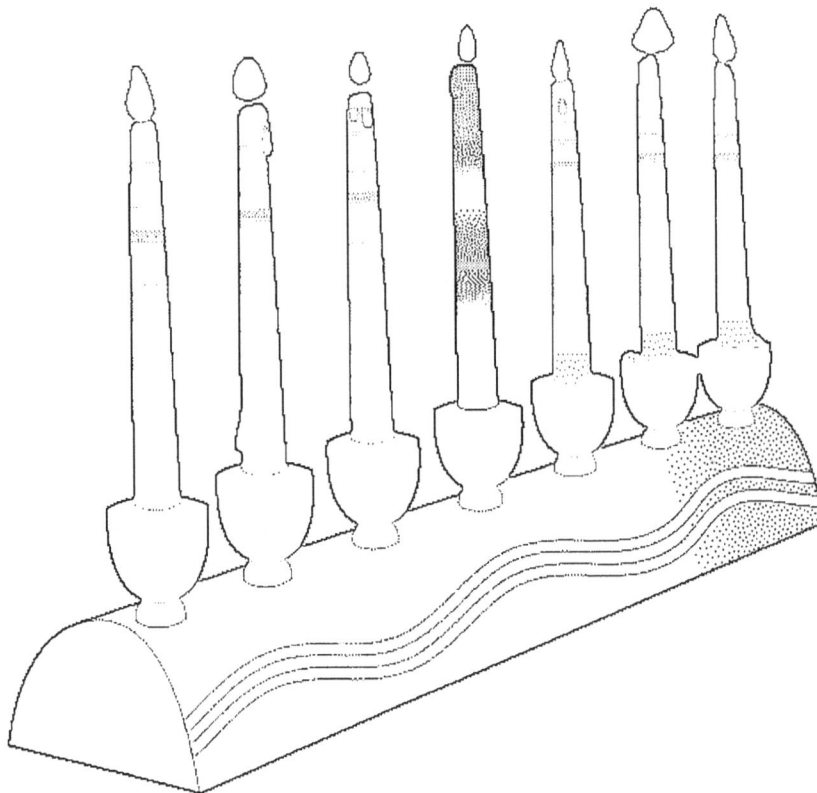

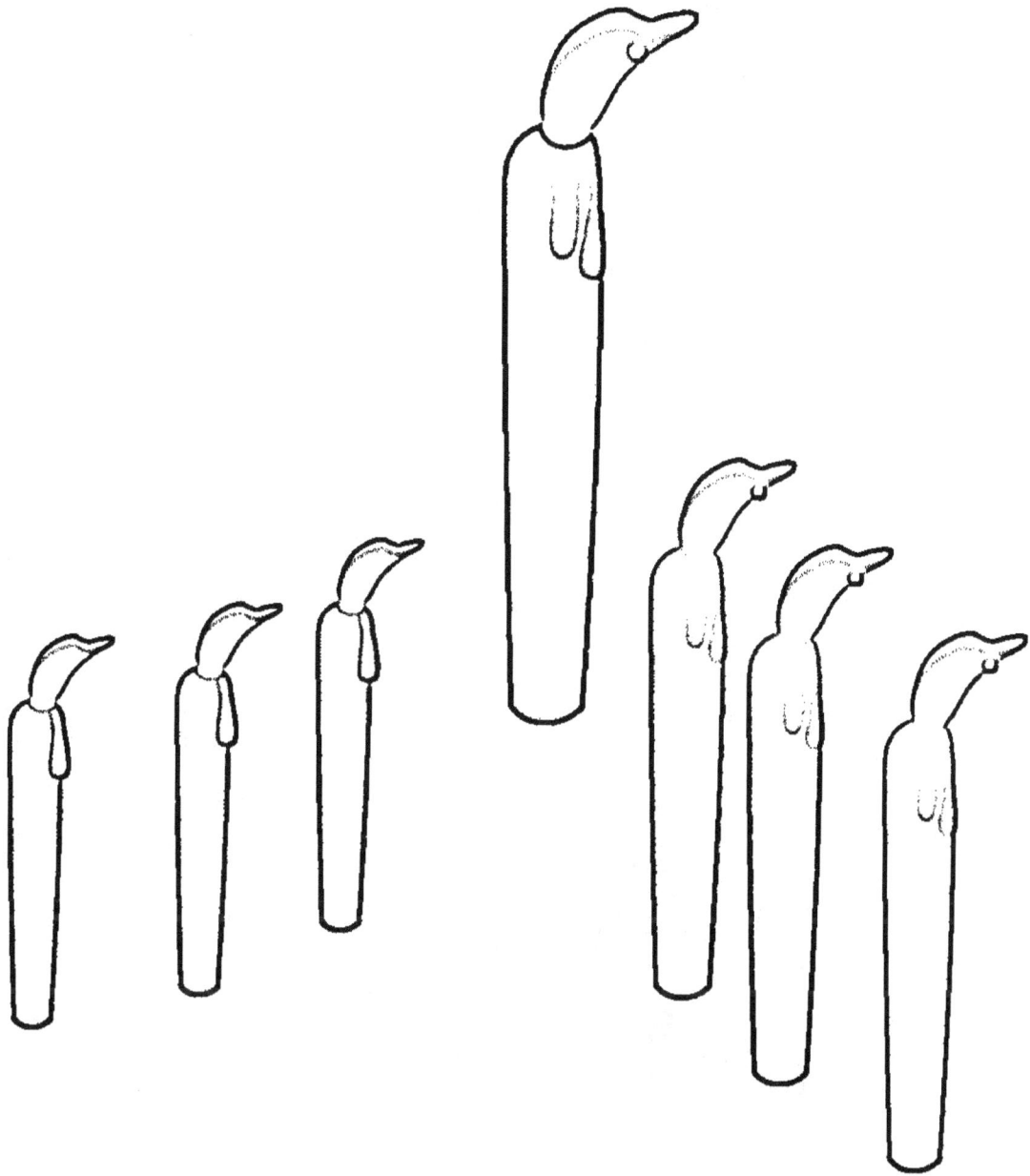

Mishumaa Saba

Nguzo Saba

On each of the 7 nights, a child lights one of the candles on the Kinara. A Kinara is a special candleholder used during Kwanzaa.

Each night one of the seven principles of Kwanzaa is discussed. The phrase for seven principles in Swahili is Nguzo Saba. These principles are values of African culture which contribute to building and reinforcing community among African-Americans.

Umoja

Kujichagulia

Ujima

Ujamaa

Nia

Kuumba

Imani

Umoja

Kujichagulia

Ujima

Ujamaa

Nia

Kuumba

Imani

Nguzo Saba

Umoja - Unity

The first principle is Unity: Umoja (oo-MO-jah)

Let's practice saying the Swahili word for unity slowly. (oo-MO-jah)

This principle teaches that people should strive for and maintain unity in their family, community, nation, and race.

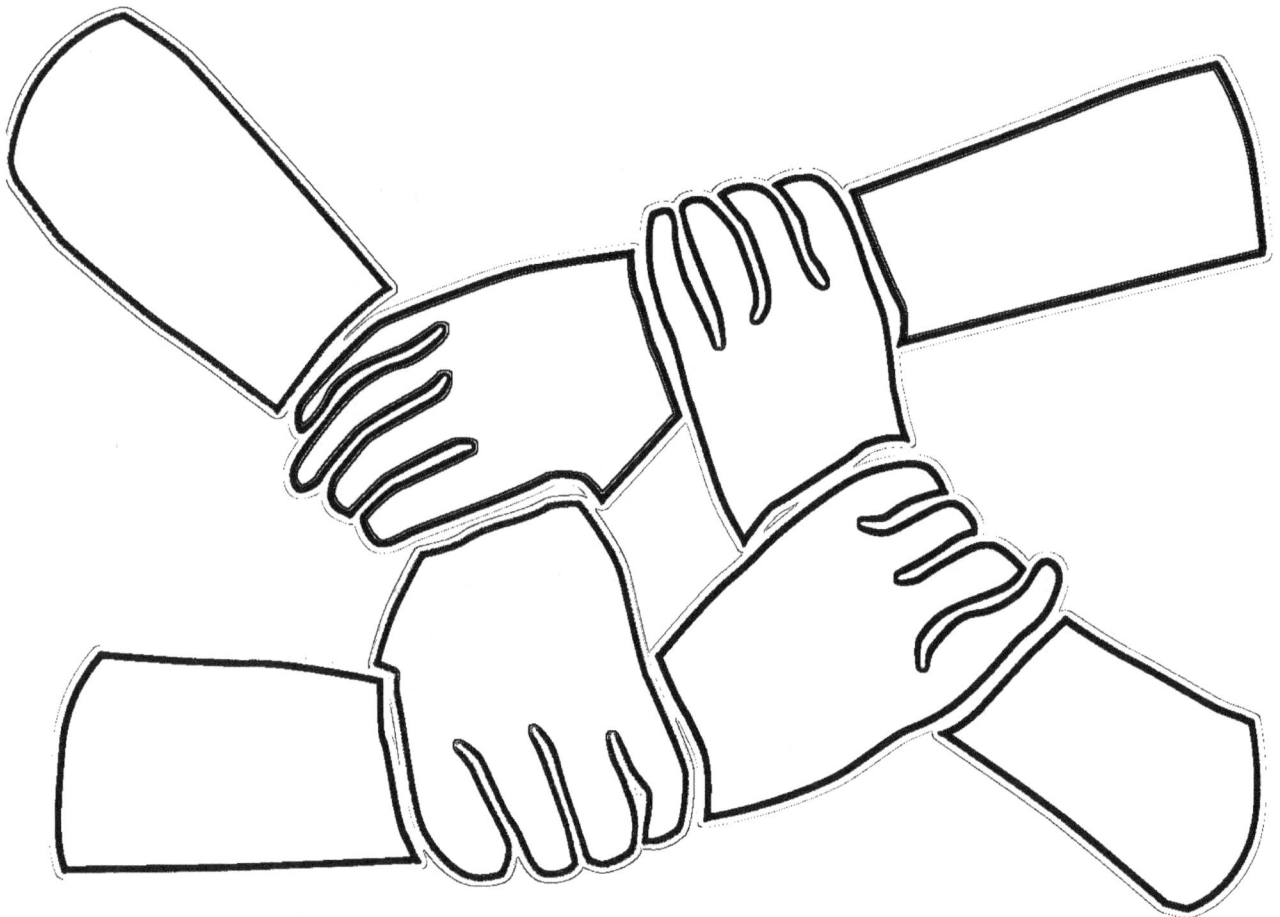

Umoja

Self-determination: Kujichagulia

The second principle is Self-determination: Kujichagulia
(koo-gee-cha-goo-LEE-yah)

To define ourselves, name ourselves, create for ourselves, and speak for ourselves.

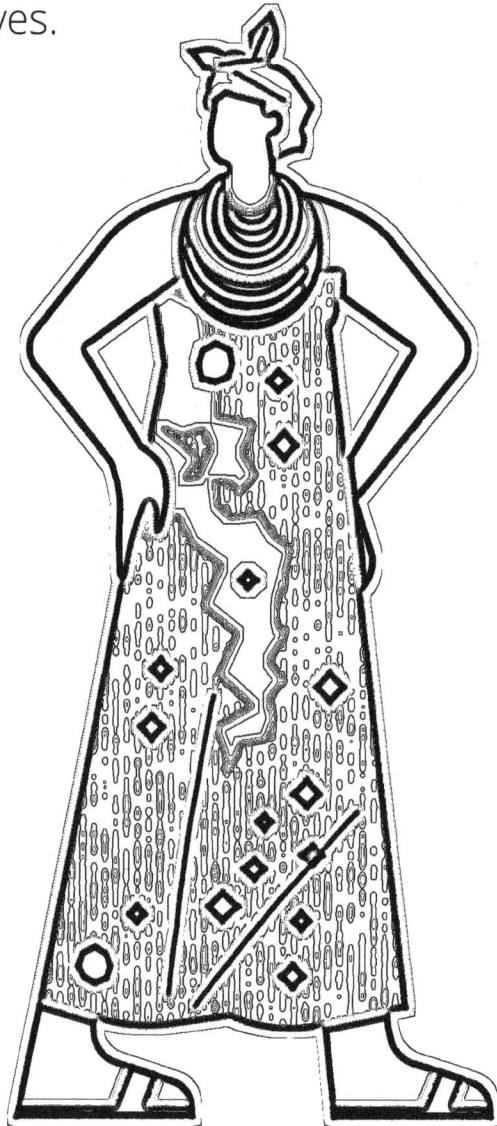

Kujichagulia

Ujima -
Collective Work and Responsibility

The third principle is Collective Work and Responsibility: Ujima. (oo-GEE-mah)

To make our brothers and sisters' problems our own and solve them together.

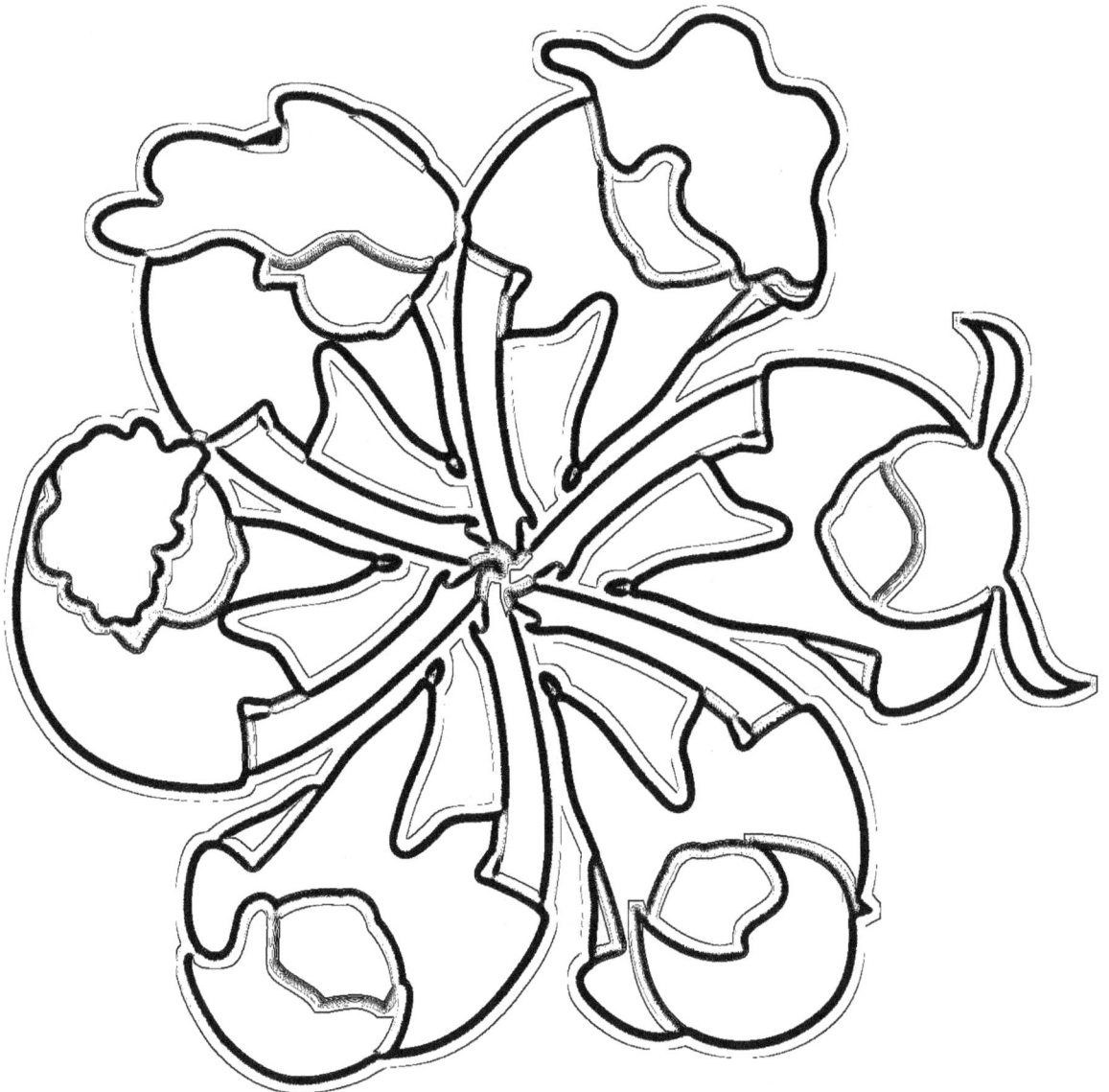

Ujima

Ujamaa
Cooperative Economics

The fourth principle is Cooperative Economics: Ujamaa

(oo-JAH-mah)

To build and maintain our own stores, shops, and other businesses and to profit from them together.

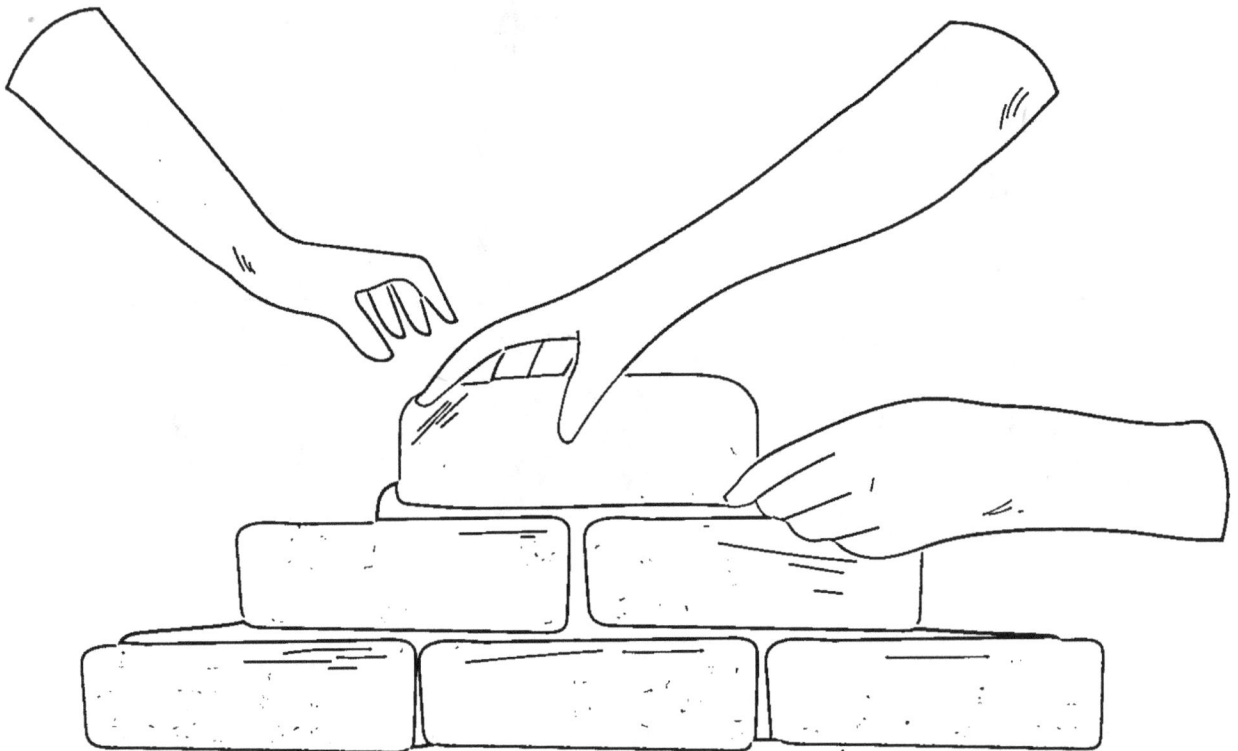

Ujamaa

Nia - Purpose

The fifth principle is Nia which means purpose. (nee-Yah)

Restore our people to their traditional greatness.

Nia

Kuumba - Creativity

The sixth principle is Creativity: Kuumba (koo-OOM-bah)
To do as much as we can to leave our community more
beautiful and beneficial than we inherited it.

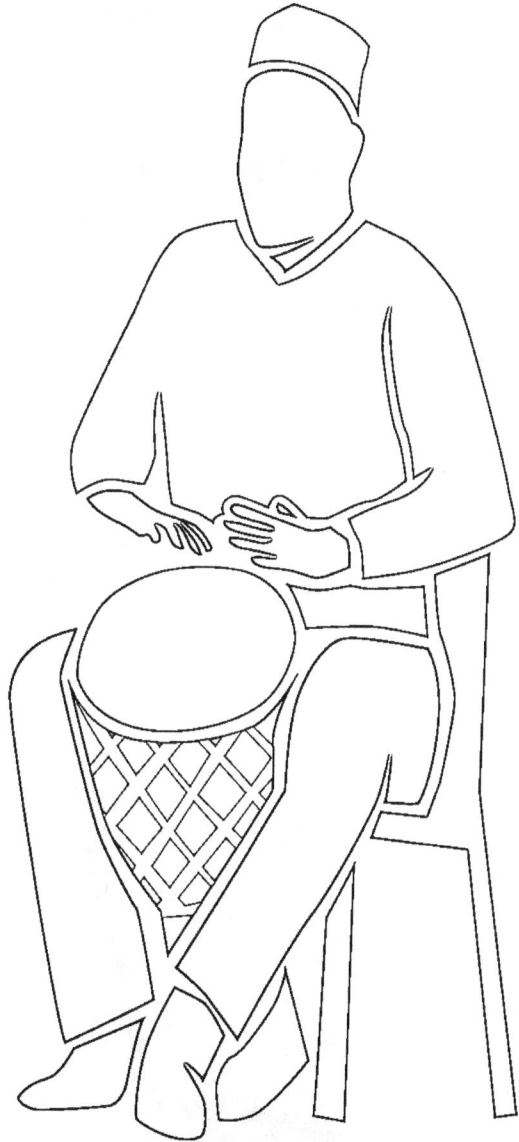

Kuumba

Imani - Faith

The seventh principle is faith: Imani (ee-MAH-nee)
To believe in your people and the righteousness of your
struggle, with all your heart. Your people are your parents,
teachers, and community leaders.

Imani

Karamu

A feast, called Karamu, is held on December 31st. Which is the day people learn about the principle of Nia (purpose).

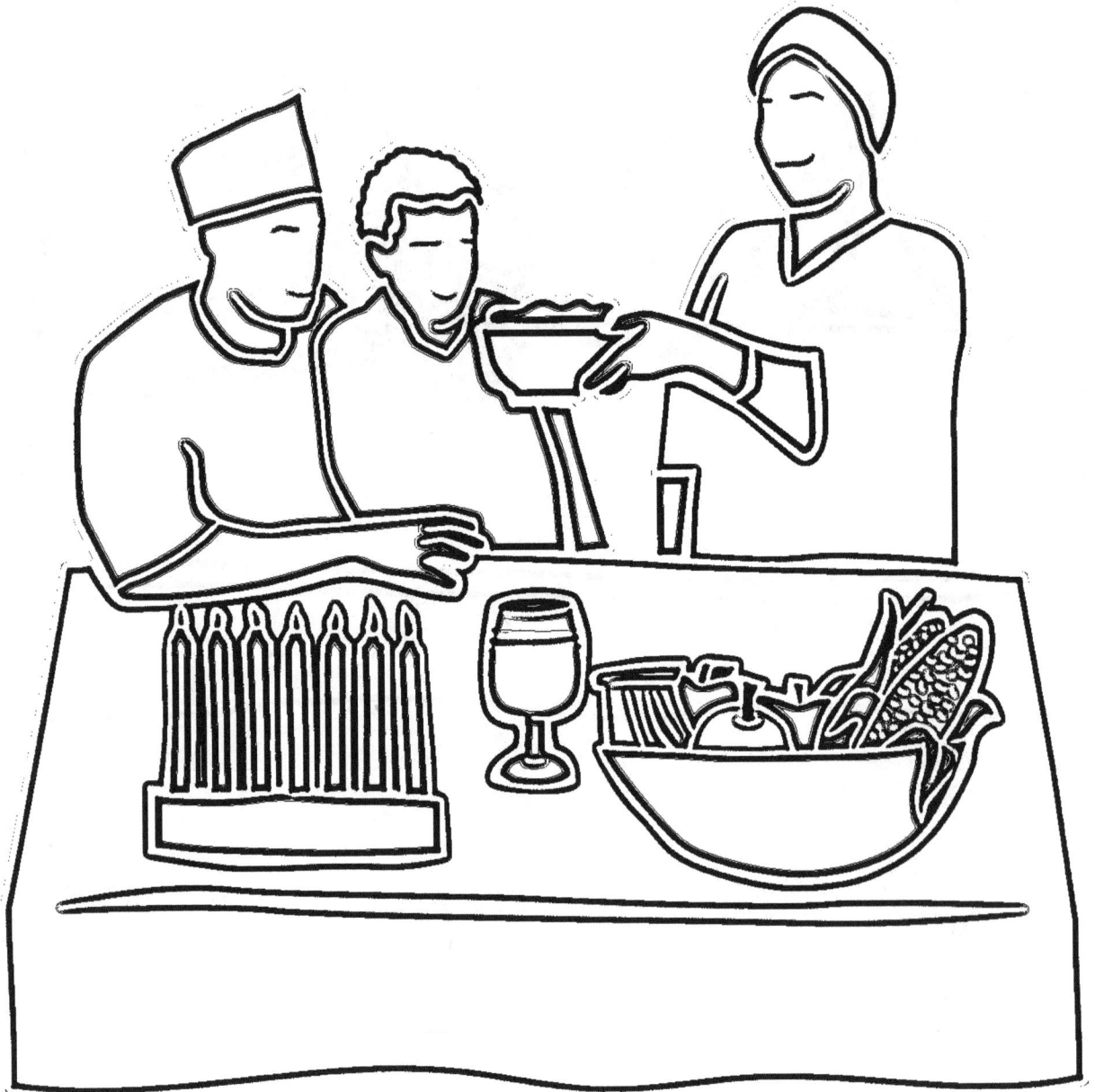

Karamu

Mkeka: Place Mat

The mkeka is made from straw or cloth. It represents the historical and traditional foundation for us to stand on and build our lives. The **mishumaa saba**, the **vibunzi**, the **mazao**, the **zawadi**, the **kikombe cha umoja**, and the **kinara** are placed directly on the mkeka.

Mkeka

Mazao: The Crops

Mazao is the Swahili word for crops (fruits, nuts, and vegetables.

Mazao

Vibunzi

Ear of Corn

One corn is called vibunzi and two are called mihindi. Each ear symbolizes a child in the family, and thus one ear is placed on the mkeka for each child. If there are no children in the family 2 mihindi are placed as each person is responsible for the children of the community.

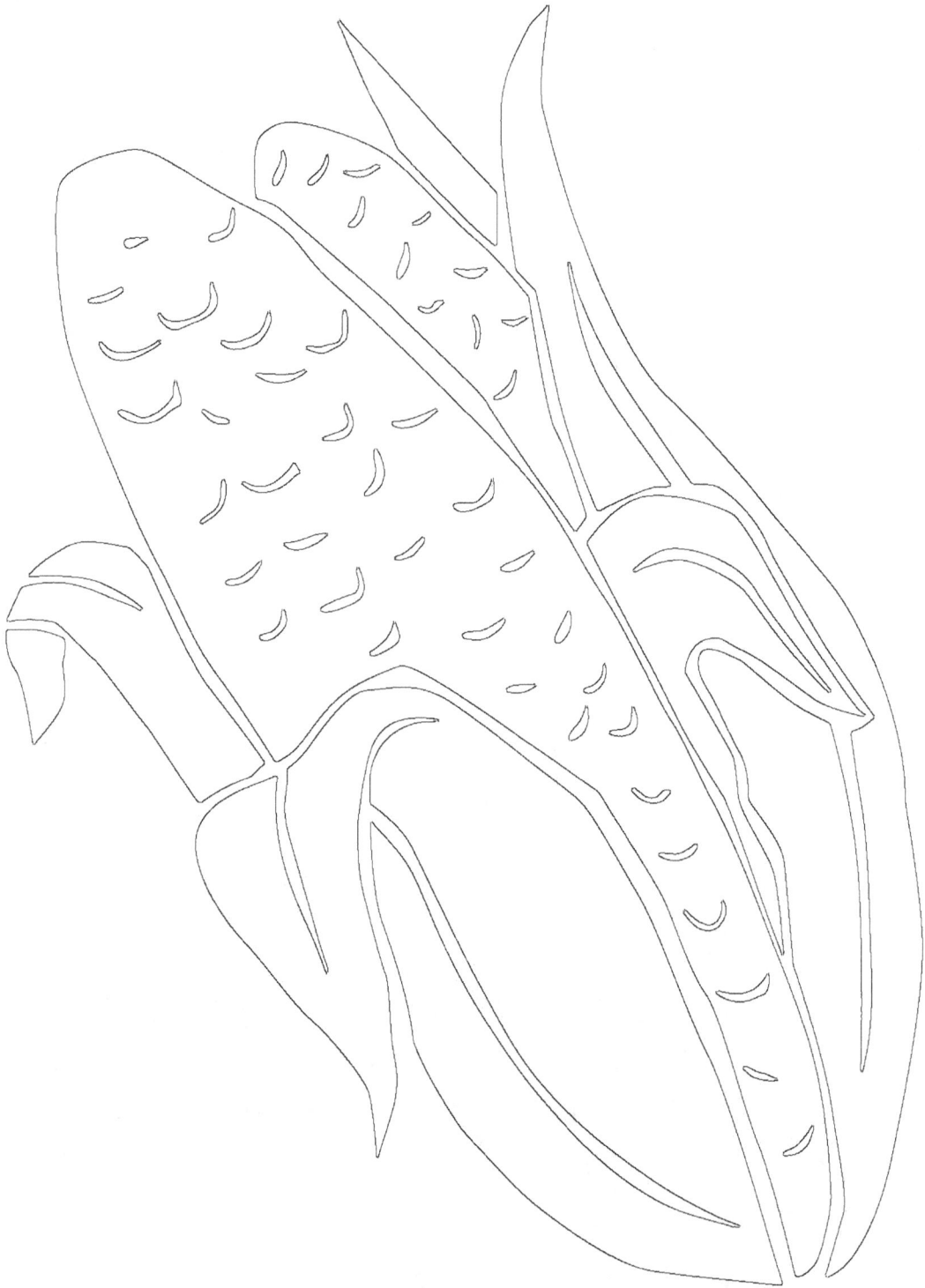

Mihindi

Zawadi: Gifts

On the 7th day of Kwanzaa (Imani), meaningful gifts are given to encourage growth, self-determination, achievement, and success.

Zawadi

Kikombe Cha Umoja
The Unity Cup

The kikombe cha umoja is a special cup that is used to perform the libation (tambiko) ritual during the karamu feast on the sixth day of Kwanzaa. The libation (water, juice, or wine) is passed around in the Kikombe Cha Umoja for each person to sip. The last of the libation is poured out by the elders to give to the ancestors.

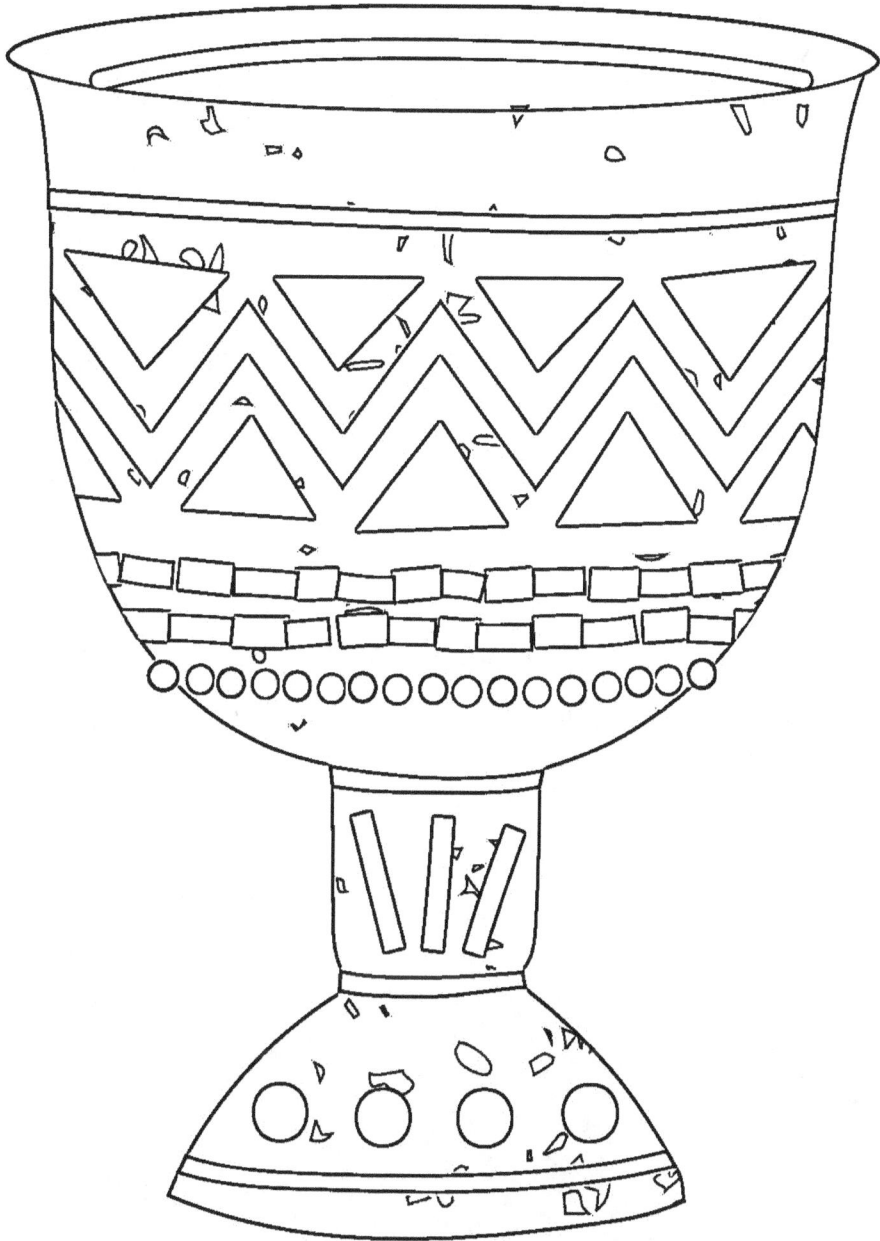

Kikombe Cha Umoja

Bendara
Red, Black, and Green Flag

This Bendara flag was created by pan-African leader Marcus Garvey. The flag consist of 3 stripes: 1 red, 1 black, and 1 green.

Red represents the struggle for self-determination and freedom for people of color.

The color black in the flag represents the people, the earth's soil, the source of life and represents the opening and closing of doors.

Green represents the earth that sustains our lives and provides hope, divination, employment, and the fruits of the harvest.

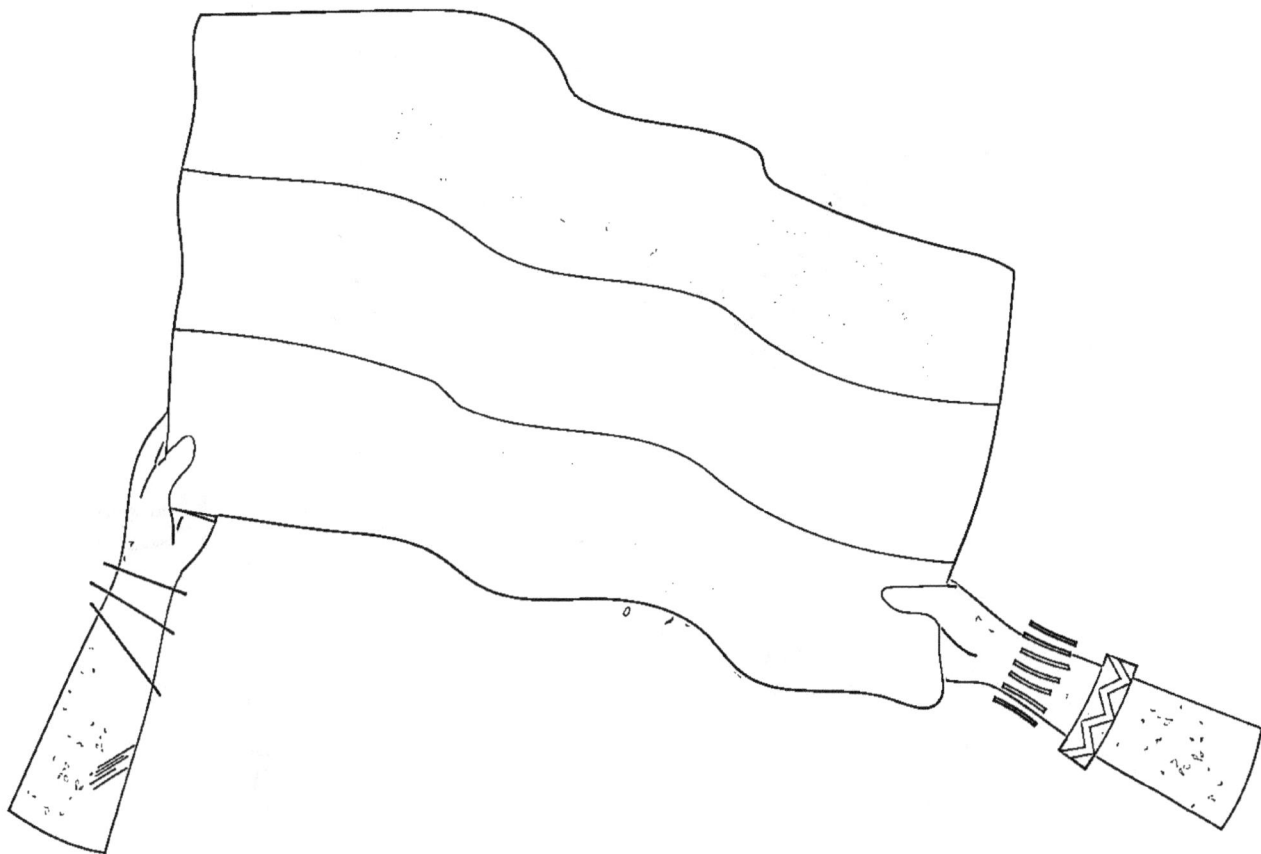

Bandana

kucheza   -   Dance

kucheza - Dance

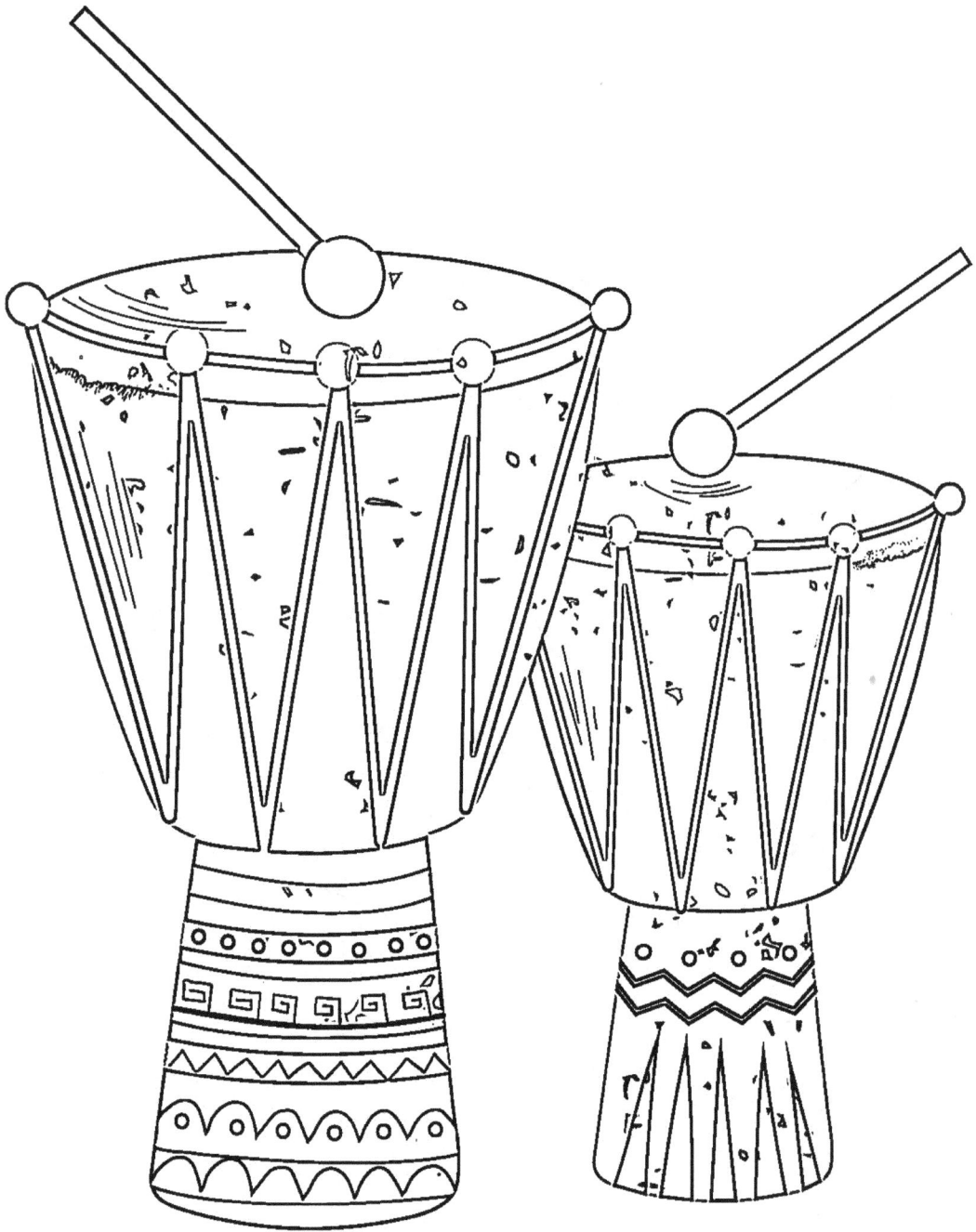

Drums - Ngoma

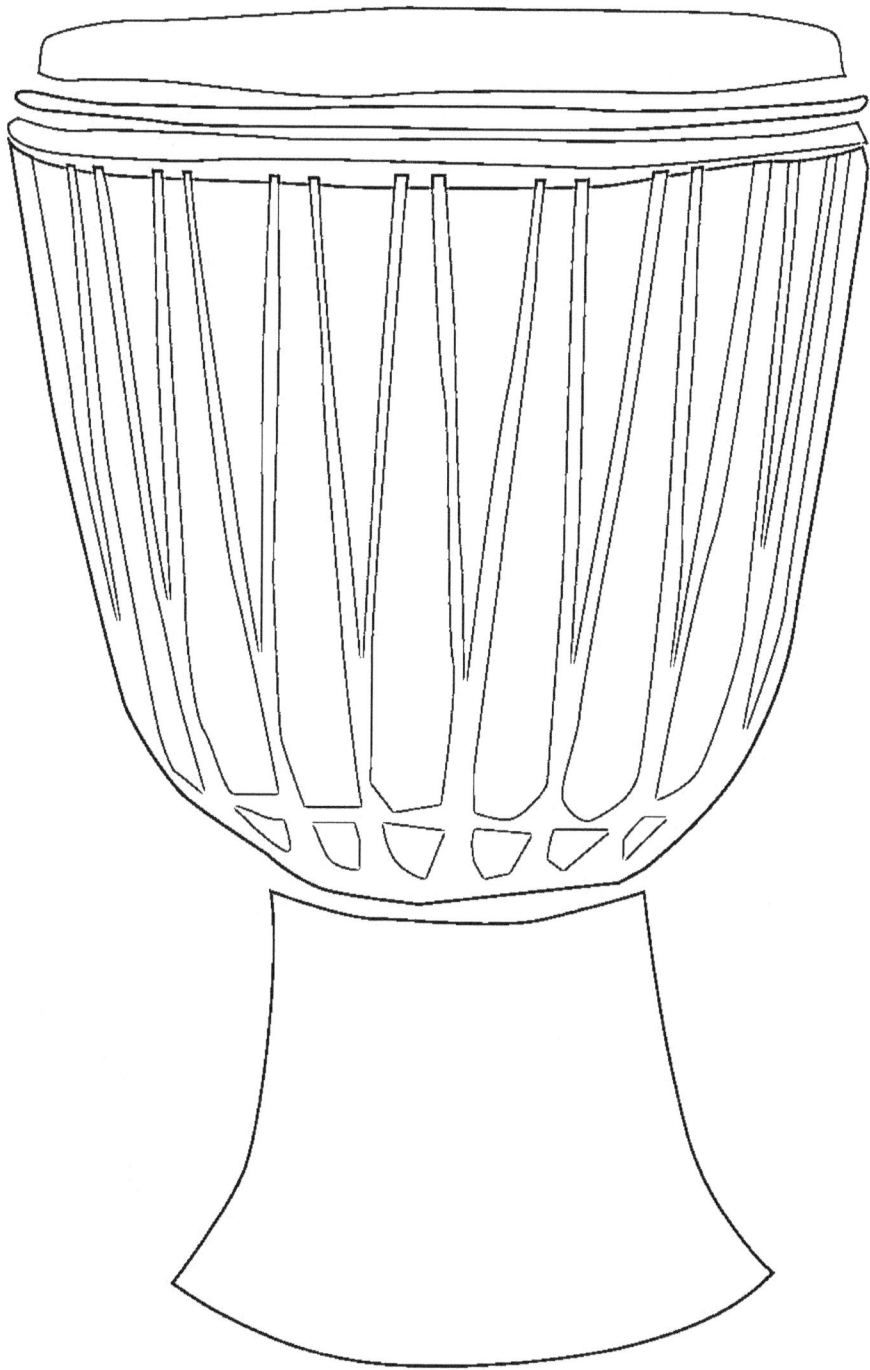

Drums - Ngoma

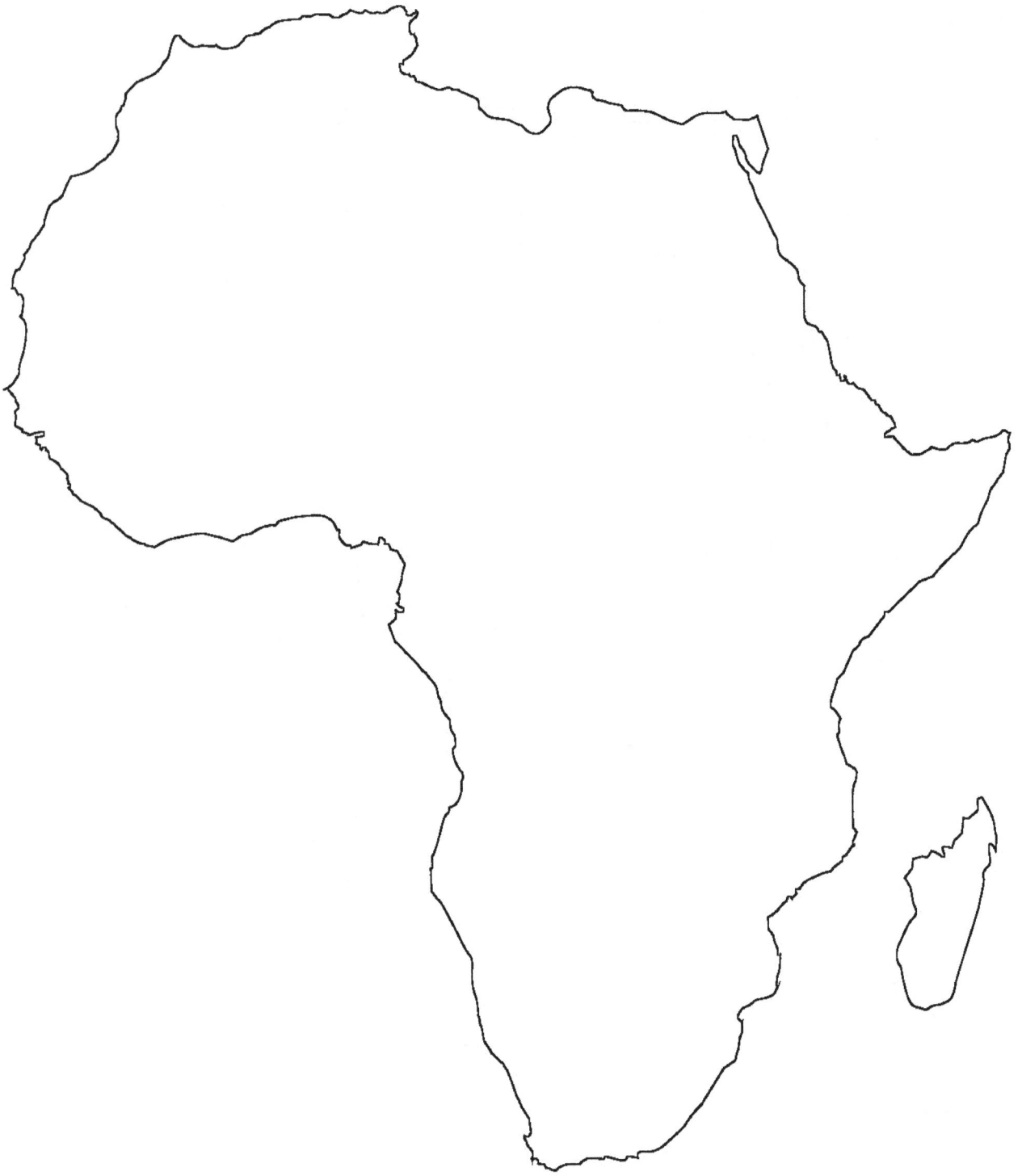

Africa